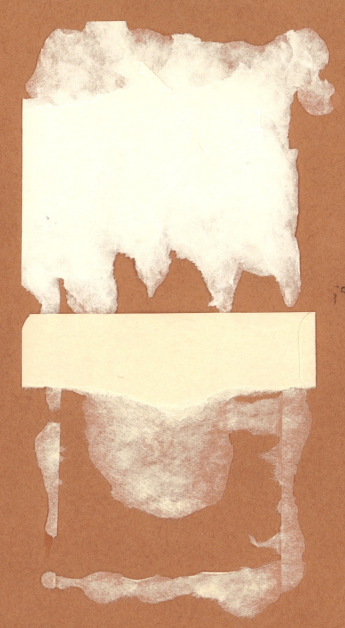

ABOUT OWLS

FOUR WINDS PRESS · NEW YORK

ABOUT OWLS

written by **MAY GARELICK**   illustrated by **TONY CHEN**

Author's Note

Someone asked me why I chose the particular owls. In choosing
the Elf Owl (the smallest), the Barn Owl (middle sized), and
the Great Horned Owl (one of the biggest), I considered size as
well as habits and habitat.
I hope to explain the habits and general characteristics of all
owls by telling the stories of the life style and habits of these
three owls.

LIBRARY OF CONGRESS CATALOGING IN PUBLICATION DATA
Garelick, May.
About owls.
SUMMARY: Describes the characteristics and habits of various species of owls.
1. Owls—Juvenile literature. [1. Owls] I. Title. QL696.S8G37   598.9'7   74–31324 ISBN 0–590–07389–3

Published by Four Winds Press, A Division of Scholastic Magazines, Inc., New York, N.Y. Text copyright
© 1975 by May Garelick. Illustrations copyright © by Anthony Chen. All Rights Reserved. Printed in the
United States of America. Library of Congress Catalog Card Number: 74–31324.

2   3   4   5   79   78   77   76

Have you ever seen an owl? Sometimes you can see one in the daytime. But the best time to see an owl is at night. When night comes and the daytime birds are asleep, owls are awake.

One night you may hear a screech, a squawk, a hoot, or a whooo. If you do, you will know that an owl is near. Soon it will hunt for something to eat. Big owls look for snakes, rabbits, mice, skunks, or oppossum. Little owls eat crickets, beetles, moths, grasshoppers, or any insects they can find.

It is nighttime in the desert. Soon an owl will come out of his home in this cactus plant. Here he comes. A little Elf Owl.

He's looking for something to eat. He's looking for insects.

Be very quiet. Because if he hears you, he may put one of his wings up in front of his face and freeze like a statue.

Something has frightened him. And to fool his enemy he flies up to a branch and remains motionless. Now the Elf Owl looks as if he is part of the branch. He'll stay fixed to the branch until it is safe to move again. This trick of freezing like a statue helps protect him from his enemies.

The Elf Owl has still another trick. If he is captured, he lies
still and pretends he is dead until his enemy leaves. Then
he continues to hunt for food.

He hunts and eats, off and on, until dawn when he flies back to his home in the cactus and goes to sleep.

That may be why people call him an Elf Owl. Like elves, these owls are little, and like elves, mischievous.

Have you ever seen a real live owl? You don't have to go to the desert to see one.

Some owls live in the hollows of trees, some live in caves, some live in gullies. There are even owls living in church steeples, in old houses, or in abandoned barns.

If you are near a woods some night you may hear a weird, hissing scream. That's the call of a Barn Owl.

Here's a mother Barn Owl standing on the beam of an abandoned barn. She's looking for something to eat. She swivels her head fast, from side to side. She looks around. She listens. She hears something.

A mouse—hiding in a clump of grass, peers out. The owl sees the glimmer of light from the mouse's eyes. She rises quietly in the air. And because owls have soft feathers at the edges of their wings, the mouse cannot hear the owl coming. On her noiseless wings the owl swoops down and grabs the mouse.

And that is how the Barn Owl will spend the night. Looking, listening, and hunting mice. Barn Owls are always hungry and it takes a lot of mice to satisfy them.

Big owls and small owls – they all look different. Some are gray, some are brown, and some are white.

Some owls have tufts of feathers that stick up over their heads, like horns. Others have hardly any tufts at all. Hidden below these feathers are their ears. Though their ears are invisible, owls can hear the smallest sound. They hunt by listening.

You can't see their ears, but you can certainly see their big, round eyes. All other birds' eyes are on the side of their heads, but owls' eyes are set in front of the face, like ours. Yet they can't move their eyes the way we do. They can't look up or down, or from side to side without turning their heads. Their neck muscles are strong, and their necks can bend like rubber. An owl can swivel its head around so fast it looks as if it is turning in a complete circle.

Owls look different, they make different sounds, and they live in different places all over the world. In warm countries, in cold lands, in hot places, owls live where they can find their kind of food.

There are many different size owls. The smallest is the Elf Owl. As small as a sparrow, the Elf Owl could fit in your hand. The Barn Owl is a middle-sized owl, about as big as a crow. And one of the biggest, most powerful owls is the Great Horned Owl.

To get an idea of how big the Great Horned Owl is, stretch your arms out sideways, as far as you can. Your stretch probably comes to 46 or 48 inches. If your stretch reaches 55 inches it is as wide as the wing span of the Great Horned Owl.

Called "Great" because of its tremendous size and "Horned" because its tufts look like horns, it is called the "Tiger of the Air" because the Great Horned Owl is such a powerful hunter.

This Tiger of the Air makes its nest deep in the woods. At the moment a Great Horned Owl is perched on a dead tree stump, getting ready to hunt for food. He stares into the night. He sits and listens. He listens for the sound that will tell him where to find his meal.

Over there in the dry leaves a snake is asleep, hidden from other animals. You can't see the snake, can you?

The Great Horned Owl cannot see it either. The night is dark. The snake is safely hidden. After a while there's a rustle of leaves. The snake moves.

The owl hears that little sound and flies down from his perch. Swiftly and silently, the owl pounces on the snake.

The snake tries desperately to wriggle away from the owl. The snake moves fast, but the owl holds it firmly in his sharp claws—his hooked talons. It is impossible for the snake to escape.

At the same time another owl has heard the commotion below and flies down from her perch. She tries to seize the snake. The first owl puffs himself up to twice his size. He looks so big and frightening, he scares her away. Now he can settle down to eat the snake.

The second owl flies off to do her own hunting. She might swoop down on a sleeping crow. Or wait for an opposum or a skunk. She waits.

A skunk passes by. With a swift silent dive the owl lunges
at the skunk. The skunk sprays her with its defensive
weapon – an awful smell. But most birds have no sense of
smell. Neither does the owl. She captures the skunk and
eats it.

Owls have to do a lot of hunting. Especially when their
babies are hatched. They have to hunt for themselves and
for their hungry owlets.

See the four baby owls? Some are small and some are larger. The biggest one hatched out five or six days before the others. The growing owlets are always hungry. But they are too young to hunt. So the mother and father owls hunt for their babies, bring them their food, and feed them until the owlets can hunt for themselves. That is why parent owls have to hunt so much.

Whatever owls catch for food, they eat the whole thing — skin, bones, fur and all. Then hours later, they cough up balls of fur, feathers, and bones. These coughed-up wads are called pellets. If you find these pellets on the ground, you can be sure that an owl lives somewhere near.

Though nighttime is when owls are awake, sometimes an owl will come out during the day. If it sees you – owls do see by day – it might pull back into its hollow or fly away. But you won't often see an owl in the daytime unless a flock of crows has discovered the owl.

Crows are the enemies of owls. When a crow sees an owl he sends out a call. And from near and far, other crows come to join him. Pretty soon there will be a crowd of crows cawing and calling. This mob of crows swirls angrily around the owl to frighten it, and drive it away.

But the owl fights back. Remember how the owl puffed himself up to scare the other owl away from the snake? That's just what this one does now. She puffs herself up to twice her size. She looks so ferocious and frightening, she scares the crows away.

But the crows will be back. They will pester and mob an owl whenever they see one. Crows are afraid of owls. They are afraid that owls will capture them while they are asleep. So they try to drive the owls out of their territory.

But luckily for the owls this doesn't happen often. Usually owls are asleep and hidden by day, so the crows can't find them easily. And the crows are lucky, too. Their mobbing and pestering does keep the owls away from them.

Crows don't like owls and there are people who don't like owls either. The owls' weird hoots and wild screams frighten some people. They say that owls are bad luck. This is just a superstition. It is not true. Actually, by killing mice and skunks and insect pests, owls are useful. Most people like owls.

But whether they like them or not, everyone says that owls are wise.

> A *wise old owl sat in an oak.*
> *The more he saw, the less he spoke.*
> *The less he spoke, the more he heard.*
> *Why can't we all be like that wise old bird?*

This poem was written a long, long time ago. And to this day, people still say that owls are wise.

Yet other birds do all that owls do. Other birds hunt for food, lay eggs, protect and feed their young. Then why do we say that OWLS are wise?

Do we say they are wise because we like them, because they look wise, or because they seem mysterious? Do their big, round eyes make us think they are wise? Are owls really wise? How wise?

Wise enough to know what they have to know. Wise enough for an owl. But really no wiser than other birds.